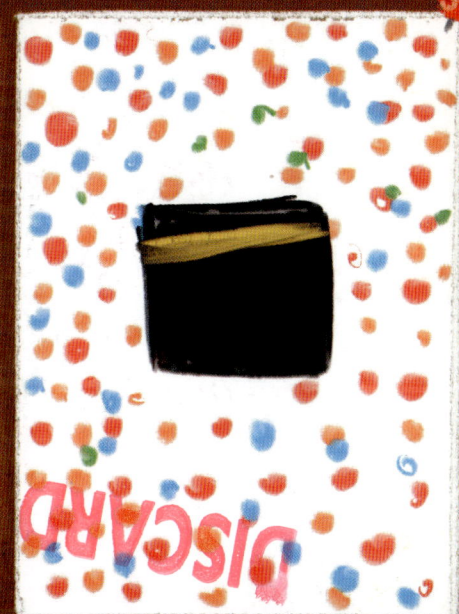

Copyright © 2020 by Al-Kisa Foundation; SABA Global

All rights reserved. First edition 2020. No part of this publication may be reproduced, distributed, or transmitted in any form or by any means, including photocopying, recording, or other electronic or mechanical methods, without the prior written permission of the publisher, except in the case of brief quotations embodied in critical reviews and certain other noncommercial uses permitted by copyright law. For permission requests, please write to the publisher at the address below.

Kisa Kids Publications
4415 Fortran Court
San Jose, CA 95134
(260) KISA KID
(260) 547-2543
info@kisakids.org

This book belongs to:

_____

Dedication

This book is dedicated to the best human being to ever walk the earth, the Noble Prophet of Islam, Prophet Muḥammad (ṣ). May Allah give us the tawfīq to follow in his footsteps, and those of his holy progeny.

Acknowledgments

Prophet Muḥammad (ṣ): The pen of a writer is mightier than the blood of a martyr.

True reward lies with Allah, but we would like to sincerely thank Sisters Marzieh Abbas, Nida Syed, Nazeera Salak, Sabika Mithani, Michile Khan, Abeda Khimji, Iman Daroudi and Abir Rashid for their efforts.
May Allah bless them in this world and the next.

Preface

Prophet Muḥammad (ṣ): Nurture and raise your children in the best way. Raise them with the love of the Prophets and the Ahl al-Bayt ('a).

Literature is an influential form of media that often shapes the thoughts and views of an entire generation. Therefore, in order to establish an Islamic foundation for future generations, there is a dire need for compelling Islamic literature. Over the past several years, this need has become increasingly prevalent throughout Islamic centers and schools everywhere. Due to the growing dissonance between parents, children, society, and the teachings of Islam and the *Ahl al-Bayt ('a)*, this need has become even more pressing. Al-Kisa Foundation, along with its subsidiary, Kisa Kids Publications, was conceived in an effort to help bridge this gap with the guidance of *'ulamā'* and the help of educators. We would like to make this a communal effort and platform. Therefore, we sincerely welcome constructive feedback and help in any capacity.

The goal of *Hamza and Aliya Share the Ramadan Cheer* is to get children excited about an extremely special month in the Islamic calendar, as well as shed light on how to positively celebrate its arrival. The month of *Ramaḍān* is full of blessings and barakah and should be anticipated and celebrated! Muslims around the world wait for the coming of this month and use it as an opportunity to reaffirm their commitment to their Lord, through fasting, prayer, reciting the Qur'ān and self reflection. This month is a time to work on one's spiritual cleansing and self building, as well as enhancing one's social and familial bonds. This book has messages of how to incorporate positive changes into one's life by making good resolutions, eating healthy food, being a good neighbor and a contributing citizen. It also shows how families can come together and strengthen their bonds by cooking, eating and sharing food and memories. May this book bring about insight on how to positively share the *Ramaḍān* cheer!

We pray to Allah to give us the strength and *tawfīq* to perform our duties and responsibilities.

With Du'ās,
Nabi R. Mir (Abidi)

Disclaimer: Religious texts have not been translated verbatim so as to meet the developmental and comprehension needs of children.

Marḥūmīn Dedication

Please recite a Sūrah al-Fātiḥah for the Marḥūmīn of
Dharamsey Family
Gangjee Family
Dawood Nasser Family
Merchant Family

As well as
Marḥūm SultanAli Merchant
Marḥūma Zehra Merchant

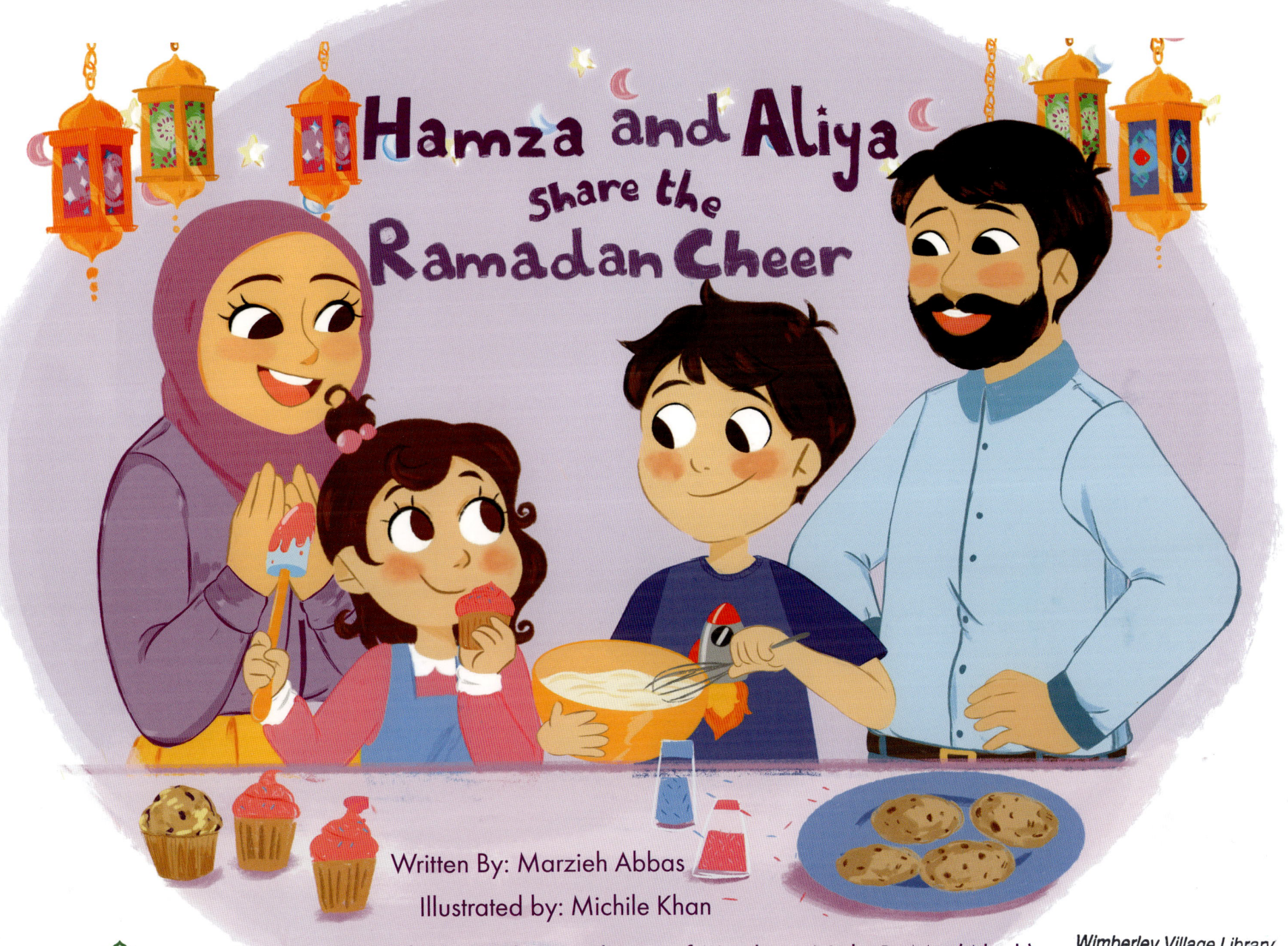

Hamza and Aliya share the Ramadan Cheer

Written By: Marzieh Abbas
Illustrated by: Michile Khan

Kisa Kids Publications | Under the Guidance of Moulana Nabi R. Mir (Abidi)

"Salāmun 'alaykum* Hamza and Aliya. Good morning! Hurry down, today is a special day!" said Mama excitedly.

* ā is an elongated "a" sound, like "aa"; 'a is a heavy "a" sound that comes from the middle of the throat

"*Wa 'alaykum salām*, Mama," Aliya and Hamza replied together, rubbing their eyes as they jumped out of bed and raced each other downstairs wondering what the special day was about.

Mama and Baba had already assembled and labeled several boxes and filled them with clothes and toys.

They had dusted and cleaned the house, rearranged the furniture, organized the fridge and put out fresh, fragrant flowers in a vase.

Mama had taken out new table mats and candles from the closet.

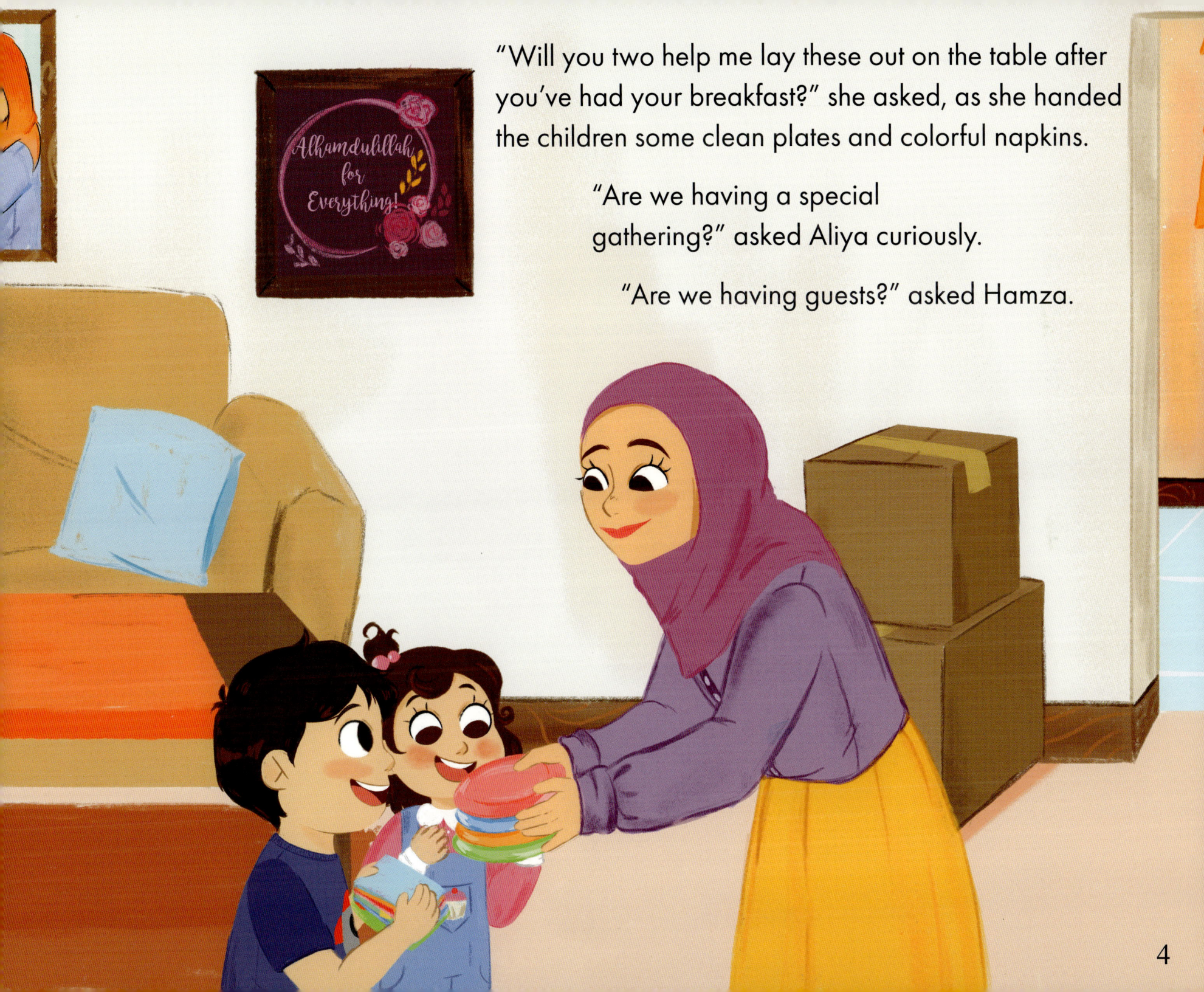

"Will you two help me lay these out on the table after you've had your breakfast?" she asked, as she handed the children some clean plates and colorful napkins.

"Are we having a special gathering?" asked Aliya curiously.

"Are we having guests?" asked Hamza.

"It *is* sort of a gathering," confirmed Baba as he stacked the boxes.

"But instead of having guests at our house, *we* are going to be the guests of **Allah!** The holy month of *Ramaḍān** is starting! We will go to look for the *Ramaḍān* moon tonight, *inshā'Allāh*."

* ḍ is a pronounced "dh"

That evening, after a little searching, they spotted the new moon signaling the start of *Shahr Ramaḍān*. They hung up a sparkly *Ramaḍān* banner, colorful lanterns, and glowing moon and star lights.

After dinner, Hamza, Aliya, and Mama sat down to hear Baba tell a story about his childhood in Pakistan. It was the same story every year, but it never lost its charm.

"When I was little, my siblings and I would accompany your grandfather to the highest roof in our neighborhood," Baba would say. "All the children in the neighborhood would search for the *Ramaḍān* moon together. The first one to spot the moon would receive a special prize. It was the best time of the year. We would wait to hear the *musarahati* in the streets at *suḥur* and would enjoy *samosas* and *jalebis* at *ifṭār*. We would make extra *duʿās* during the blessed *Nights of Qadr* and memorize some of Allah's beautiful names from *Duʿā Jawshan al-Kabīr.** We would try to be extra timely with our prayers and encourage each other to be generous and helpful. On the first day of *Ramaḍān*, your grandfather used to make each of us siblings write down at least one bad habit that we would try to eliminate over the month, and at least one good habit we would try to form during the holy month. It was always exciting to discuss our progress as the days to *Eid al-Fiṭr*** drew closer."

* ī is an elongated "e" sound, like "ee"
** ṭ is an emphasised "t" sound like the arabic letter ط

After hearing Baba's lovely story, Hamza and Aliya were inspired to write down their own resolutions for the holy month.

Next, they helped Mama decide what they would distribute at the *masjid*,

whom they would send food to,

and whom they would invite to their home to share special *Ramaḍān* meals with.

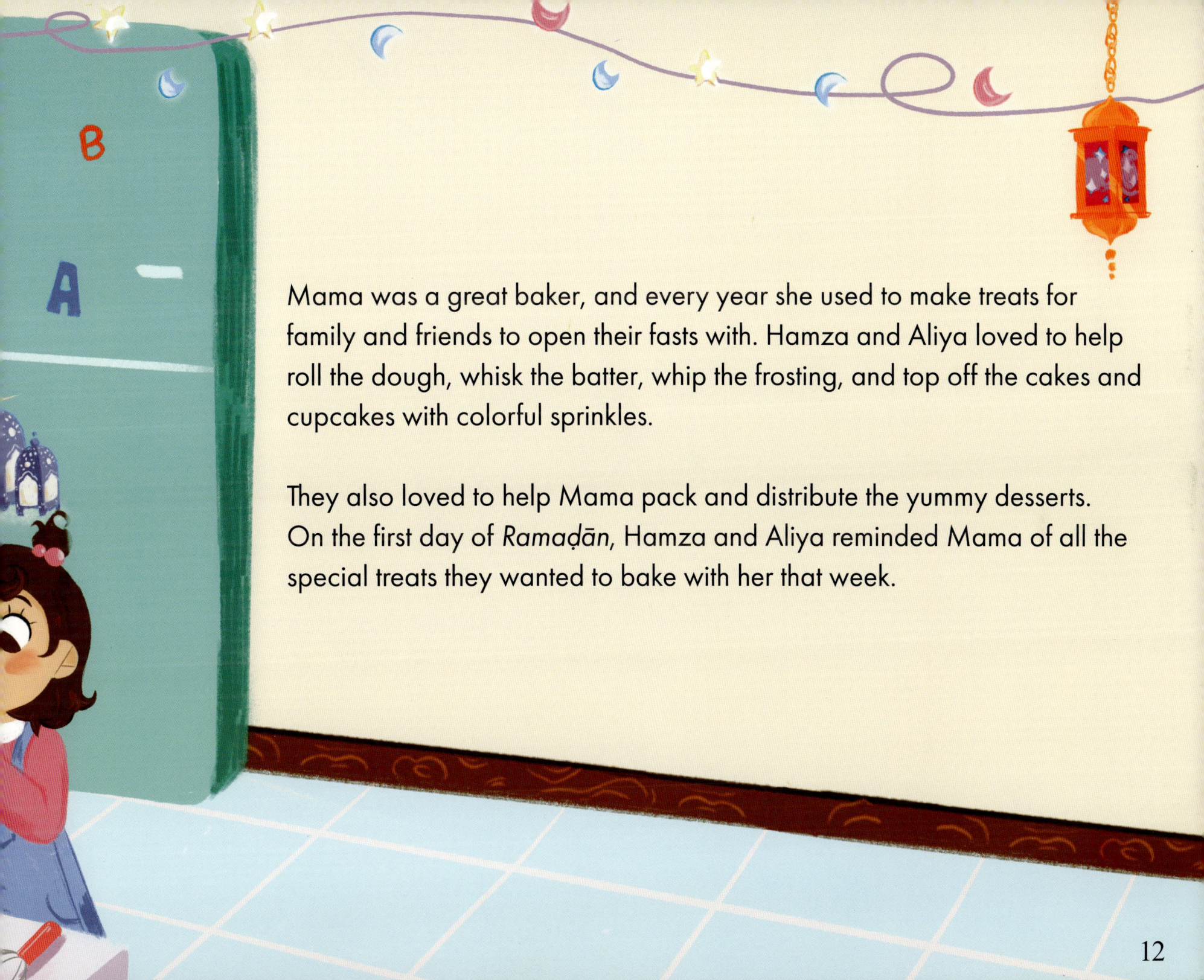

Mama was a great baker, and every year she used to make treats for family and friends to open their fasts with. Hamza and Aliya loved to help roll the dough, whisk the batter, whip the frosting, and top off the cakes and cupcakes with colorful sprinkles.

They also loved to help Mama pack and distribute the yummy desserts. On the first day of *Ramaḍān*, Hamza and Aliya reminded Mama of all the special treats they wanted to bake with her that week.

On Monday, they made scrumptious Oatmeal Raisin Cookies.

On Tuesday, they made colorful Rainbow Macarons, Aliya's favorite dessert.

On Wednesday, they baked sweet and tangy Lemon Blueberry Muffins.

THURSDAY

FRIDAY

On Thursday, they made a delicious batch of chewy Granola-Fig Bars.

On Friday, they made soft and spongy Banana Bread with walnuts and chocolate chips.

On Saturday, they made fragrant Cinnamon Rolls with Cream Cheese Frosting, Hamza's favorite dessert.

SATURDAY

On Sunday, Mama worked hard all day to prepare food to share with the neighbors.

After everything was done, she flopped onto the sofa, "Alḥamdulillāh*, we've prepared all the food. I'm going to take a quick nap now."

* ḥ is a heavy "ha" sound that comes from the middle of the throat

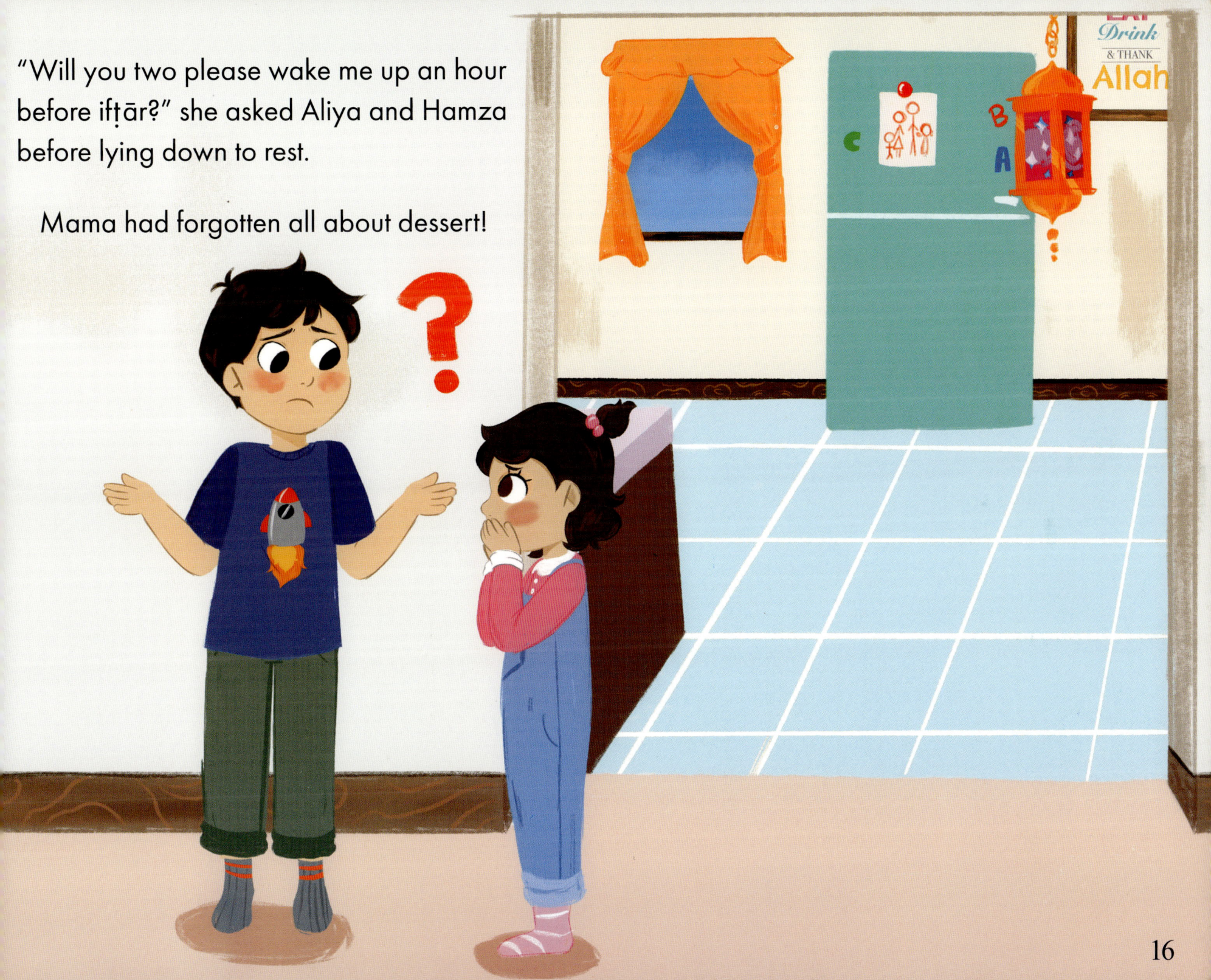

"Will you two please wake me up an hour before ifṭār?" she asked Aliya and Hamza before lying down to rest.

Mama had forgotten all about dessert!

Hamza and Aliya had an idea. They video-called their grandmother for help.

"*Salāmun 'alaykum*, Nani," said Hamza. "Mama has been working so hard all day to prepare food, she just went to take a nap. We want to bake a treat for her to open her fast with!"

"*Wa 'alaykum salām*, my dears. Hmm..." thought Nani, "What should we make?"
"We don't know how to use the oven, Nani, and we don't even have a recipe!" exclaimed Aliya.

"Oh dear!" said Nani. "How about we make a no-bake recipe instead?"
"What's that?" they asked curiously.

"It's a treat you can make without having to bake," explained Nani.
"Yummm, we can manage that!" said Hamza and Aliya, their eyes lit up with excitement.

"Can we make a big batch to share with our neighbors if they turn out well, Nani?" asked Hamza.

"Sure," smiled Nani, nodding her head approvingly. "*Inshā'Allāh* they will turn out just perfect!"

"*Salāmun 'alaykum*, Ammi. How are you? What are you three planning?" asked Baba, coming into the room.

"Baba, Baba! Nani is telling us how to make a surprise treat for Mama!" explained Aliya.

"Mama is very tired today. She's gone for a nap and we don't want her to do any more work when she wakes up," added Hamza.

"What a great idea! Can I help too?" asked Baba.

Baba gathered the spatulas and measuring cups, and grabbed some bowls and trays.

Hamza pulled up a stool and helped Aliya climb onto the counter top.

"Don't forget to start with *Bismillāh*," reminded Nani, "You will be amazed by the barakah and blessings it will add to your treat!"

They measured.

They poured.

They peeled.

They mashed and they mixed.

They rolled and they dipped.

Nani guided them all the way.

"Ta-da!" exclaimed Aliya.

"Alḥamdulillāh!" said Nani. "That's our energy-packed, superfood date balls all done!"

"What's a superfood, Nani?" asked Hamza, as he helped Aliya lay out the carefully rolled date balls in a tray.

"Superfoods are fruits, grains, and vegetables that are packed with healthy nutrients that boost your brain power and energy levels. Prophet Muḥammad (ṣ) loved these foods and many of them are mentioned in the Qur'ān as well!"

"Then these will be just right for Mama to open her fast with!" said Aliya as she nibbled on the yummy leftovers in the bowl.

"Māshā'Allāh! You are such a good girl, never letting anything go to waste," praised Nani. "There's only an hour until ifṭār time," said Hamza. "JazākAllāh for your help Nani, Khuda haafiz."

As their call ended, Aliya said, "Now it's time to wake Mama up."

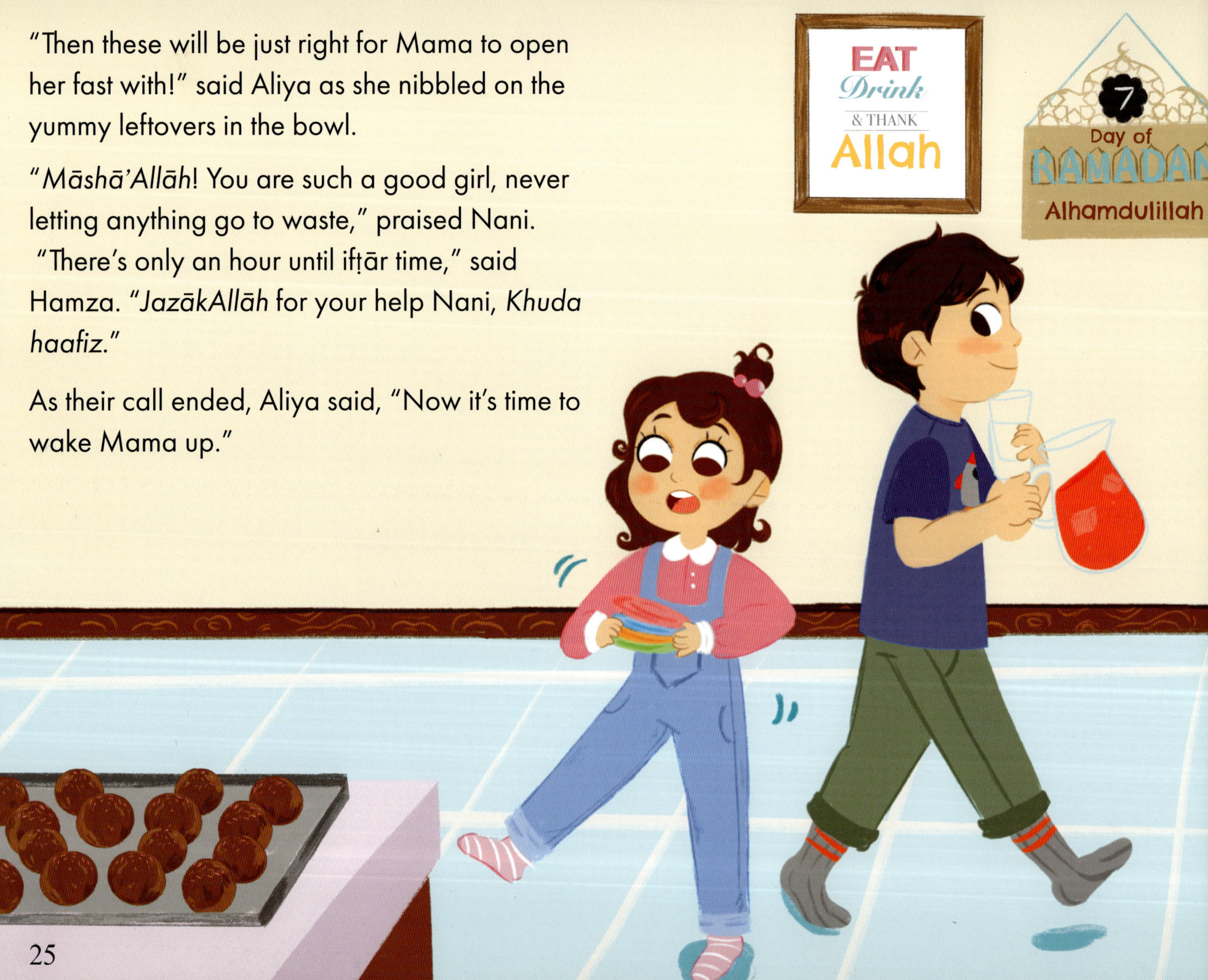

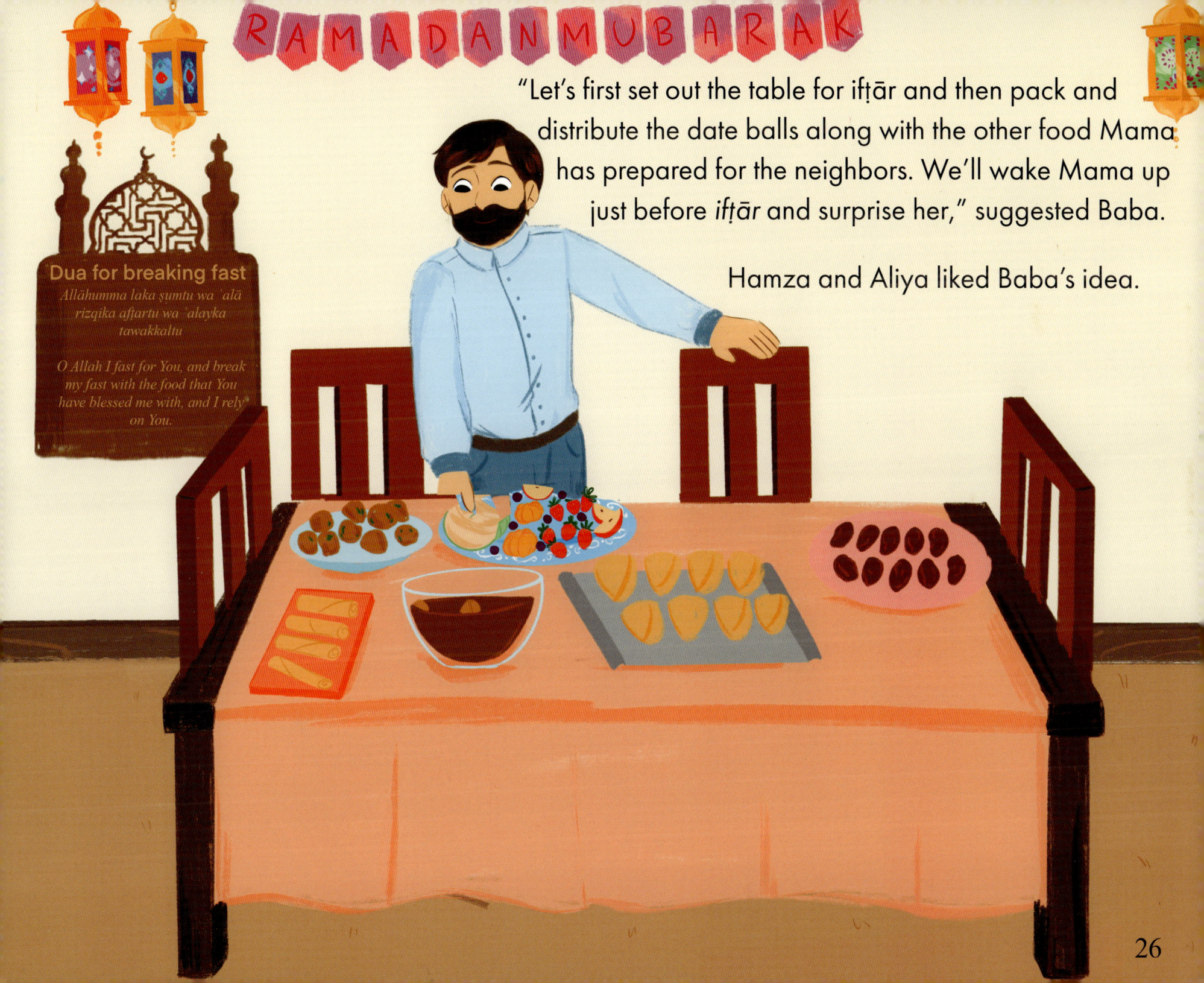

"Let's first set out the table for ifṭār and then pack and distribute the date balls along with the other food Mama has prepared for the neighbors. We'll wake Mama up just before *ifṭār* and surprise her," suggested Baba.

Hamza and Aliya liked Baba's idea.

Dua for breaking fast
Allāhumma laka ṣumtu wa ʿalā rizqika afṭartu wa ʿalayka tawakkaltu

O Allah I fast for You, and break my fast with the food that You have blessed me with, and I rely on You.

They found some fancy ribbons and pretty boxes and filled each box with date balls and headed out to distribute them to their neighbors.

يَا خَيْرَ الرَّازِقِينَ

In the meantime, Mama woke up to an empty house. She panicked when she saw the dusky sky and she realized that the food trays for the neighbors had disappeared too!

"Mama, Mama! *Salāmun 'alaykum*. The neighbors were so happy when we gave them their food trays. And guess what we made for you?"

"Cake pops?" Mama tried to guess.

"Nope," said Aliya.

"*Bismillāh*, go on, try some," urged Baba. So Mama said Bismillāh and recited a short *du'ā* to thank Allah for all of His blessings, and opened her fast with one of the truffle-like date balls.

"*Māshā'Allāh*! These are fantastic! Mmm, what did you put in it?" asked Mama, as she popped another one into her mouth.

"It's a secret recipe," giggled Aliya and Hamza.

Ding_Dong

Entering the house
My Lord. Make me enter into good, and go forth into good, and help me with Your Power.

Leaving the house
In the name of Allah, I believe in Allah, I rely on Allah. That which Allah wills takes place. There is no power nor strength but in Allah.

"*Salāmun 'alaykum!* Surprise! I thought my little chefs would like some date ball taste-testers," laughed Nani. "So we came over to join you for *iftār!*"

"*Alḥamdulillāh,*" said Mama. "Thank you Allah, for blessing me with a wonderful family."

Energy Date Balls

Would you like to try Nani's secret recipe for energy date balls?

Here is what you will need:
- 3 cups of pitted dates
- 1 tsp chia seeds (if you like)
- 3 tsp honey
- 1 cup of ground almonds
- 1 cup finely shredded coconut
- 3 tsp cocoa powder
- 2 tsp of rainbow sprinkles (Aliya insisted Nani add this to her recipe)

This is what you have to do:
Soak the dates in warm water for 2-3 minutes.
Drain the water.
Combine the drained dates with honey, chia seeds, ground almonds and cocoa powder.
Put the mixture into a food processor and blend, or, you can mix it together using a fork instead.
Once everything is mixed well, roll a small amount of the mixture into a small ball and coat it with either finely shredded coconut, cocoa powder or sprinkles.
You can also put the balls on lollipop sticks and dip them in melted chocolate. Don't forget to make a list of all the people you want to share your yummy date balls with!

Macarons

Ingredients:

3 egg whites (at room temperature)
¼ cup castor sugar
pinch of salt
¼ tsp cream of tartar
2 drops food coloring
1 cup almond flour
2 cups powdered sugar

Instructions:

- ◊ Preheat your oven to 280°F/140°C.
- ◊ Beat the egg whites in a stand mixer until foamy. Then add a pinch of salt, cream of tartar and castor sugar. Beat for another 10 minutes till the mixture forms stiff peaks.
- ◊ Add food coloring.
- ◊ In a separate bowl, sift the almond flour and powdered sugar.
- ◊ Fold the dry and wet ingredients together in about 70 strokes of your spatula.
- ◊ Transfer batter into a pastry bag.
- ◊ Pipe 1 inch rounds onto a baking tray lined with parchment paper.
- ◊ Tap the tray hard to release air bubbles.
- ◊ Let the macaron tray sit out for 20-30 minutes till the tops dry.
- ◊ Bake at 280°F/140°C for 15 minutes.
- ◊ Cool the macaron shells and fill with store-bought icing.

Oatmeal Raisin Cookie

Ingredients

1 ½ cups soaked raisins
1 ½ cups all purpose flour
½ tsp salt
½ tsp baking powder
1 tsp cinnamon powder
8 oz unsalted butter, softened
1 cup light brown sugar
1 cup white sugar
2 eggs
3 cups rolled oats

Instructions

◊ Preheat your oven to 350°F /180°C.

◊ Sift flour, salt, baking powder and cinnamon powder in a bowl.

◊ Using a stand mixer or electric mixer, beat the butter until creamy. Then beat in the white and brown sugars until fluffy.

◊ Beat in eggs (one at a time) until incorporated.

◊ Pour the dry ingredients into the wet ingredients and mix together using a wooden spoon

◊ Stir in the oats and raisins. Mix.

◊ Using an ice cream scoop, form 2" balls (16 - 20) and place onto greased baking tray 4" apart.

◊ Bake for 15 minutes at 350°F /180°C.

No Bake Granola Bars

1. 1 cup of rice krispies, 2 cups of oats — Mix!

2. 1/4 cup of honey, 1/3 cup brown sugar, 1/4 cup of butter — Mix well!

3. 1/2 tsp. vanilla, add chopped figs

4. Add choc chips

5. rest for 2 hours! Enjoy!

No Bake Granola Bars

Ingredients

1 cup rice krispies
2 cups of oatmeal
¼ cup honey
¼ cup of butter
½ tsp vanilla
⅓ cup brown sugar
chopped figs
chocolate chips

Instructions

◊ Mix the oatmeal and rice krispies in a bowl.

◊ Add brown sugar, honey and butter in a pot and cook on medium-high heat until it bubbles. Then add in the vanilla and add the entire mix to the dry ingredients.

◊ Add the chopped figs into the mixture.

◊ Transfer mixture to a flat pan and evenly sprinkle chocolate chips.

◊ Let it sit for 2 hours to harden before cutting into bars.

Banana Bread

Ingredients

2 eggs
1 ¼ cups ground sugar
½ cup oil
1 tsp vanilla essence
2 tbsp yogurt
4 mashed bananas
1 ⅔ cups plain flour
1 tsp baking soda
½ tsp cinnamon powder
¼ tsp salt
½ cup chocolate chips
½ cup chopped walnuts

Instructions

◊ Preheat your oven to 350°F/180°C.

◊ Beat eggs and sugar together in a stand mixer on medium-high speed until pale.

◊ Reduce speed to low and beat in the oil.

◊ Mix in the vanilla, yogurt and mashed bananas.

◊ Sift together the flour, salt, baking soda and cinnamon together in a large bowl and keep aside.

◊ Pour the wet mixture into the dry mixture, fold well.

◊ Pour mixture into a greased loaf pan, sprinkle chocolate chips and walnuts and bake at 350°F/180°C for 1 hour.

◊ Cool on a wire rack before slicing and serving.

Blueberry Lemon Muffins

1. Mix well!
   - 2/3 cups butter
   - 3/4 cups sugar
   - 1/2 cup yogurt
   - Lemon juice and zest of 1/2 a lemon
   - 1 tsp vanilla extract
   - 2 eggs

2. Mix dry ingredients
   - 2 cups flour, mix wet + dry
   - 2 tbsp baking powder
   - Blueberries

3. Place mixture into muffin tray

4. Bake in oven at 180°C for 25 mins

Blueberry Lemon Muffins

Ingredients

⅔ cup melted butter

¾ cups sugar

½ cup yogurt

2 tbsp lemon juice

zest of half a lemon

1 tsp vanilla extract

2 eggs

2 cups flour

2 tsp baking powder

1 cup blueberries

Instructions

◊ Preheat your oven to 350°F/180°C.

◊ Beat eggs, sugar, melted butter, yogurt, lemon juice, zest and vanilla extract in a bowl until combined.

◊ Sift the flour and baking powder into a large bowl and stir in the blueberries.

◊ Make a well in the center of the flour mixture and add in the wet ingredients. Mix lightly.

◊ Divide the batter between 12 muffin cases.

◊ Bake for 25 minutes at 350°F/ 180°C.

  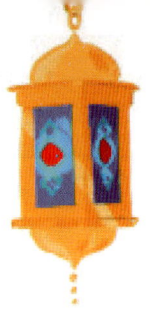 

The Prophet's (ṣ) Love for Dates and Honey

Prophet Muḥammad (ṣ) loved dates! He would tell his followers to always break their fasts with dates during Ramaḍān. It is also narrated that whenever the Prophet (ṣ) was served food that included dates, he always started with the dates!
(Mustadrak al-Wasā'il, Vol. 16, Hadīth #350 from al-Hidāyah)

The Prophet (ṣ) also liked honey. He said, "Allah has made honey a blessing. It is the cure for pains, and seventy prophets have blessed it."
(Makārim al-Akhlāq, P. 166)

 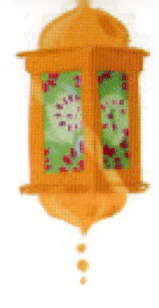  

Dates and Honey in the Qur'ān

"And We produced for you with it gardens of (date) palm trees and grapevines in which there are fruits for you from which you eat."
(Sūrah al-Mu'minūn*, Verse 19)

"And shake the trunk of the palm tree toward you; it will drop upon you fresh, ripe dates."
(Sūrah Maryam, Verse 25)

"And your Lord inspired the bee, 'Create houses for yourself in the mountains, among the trees, and [in] that which they construct. Then eat from all the fruits and follow the ways of your Lord.' There gushes from their bellies a drink of different colors, in which there is healing for people. Surely in that is a sign for people who think."
(Sūrah an-Naḥl, Verses 68-69)

* ū is an elongated "o" sound, like "oo"

Benefits of Eating Dates

In addition to being sweet and delicious, dates have a lot of nutritional benefits as well. They contain vitamins and minerals such as potassium, magnesium, copper, iron, and vitamin B. Dates are also packed full of antioxidants, which is why we call them a superfood! Antioxidants help fight things like cancer, cardiovascular disease, and Alzheimers, and lower inflammation in the body (which could otherwise cause all sorts of issues). They also promote long-term brain health!

Benefits of Honey

Honey is an antioxidant just like dates! It is anti-inflammatory, boosts your immune system, and helps with sore throats and coughs. It has vitamins and minerals such as calcium, potassium, magnesium, and vitamin B, which your body needs to keep you strong and healthy. Honey is a great, and so much healthier, alternative to sugar.

Glossary

(ṣ): Peace and blessings be upon Prophet Muḥammad (ṣ) and his family

('a): Peace and blessings be upon him/her

Ahl al-Bayt: Divinely appointed family members of Prophet Muḥammad (ṣ)

al-Fātiḥah: The first sūrah that is commonly recited and sent as a gift of prayer for the deceased

Alḥamdulillāh: All praise is for God

Allah: The Arabic term for God, a culmination of all His holy names and titles

Ammi: An urdu term that means Mother

Mama: Mother

Baba: Father

Barakah: Blessing

Bismillāh: (I begin) in the name of God

Duʿā: Supplication; a deep connection and communication between an individual and God

Duʿā Jawshan al-Kabīr: A specific duʿā commonly recited in the month of Ramaḍān, which mentions more than 1,000 names and attributes of God

Eid al-Fiṭr: The 1st day of *Shawwal* (the 10th Islamic month) that marks the end of the month of Ramaḍān and is a day of celebration for Muslims around the world

Ifṭār: The meal which is eaten at the end of one's fast after sunset

Inshā'Allāh: God-willing

Jalebi: A sweet, crispy, deep-fried dessert, popular in the South Asian subcontinent and Middle Eastern countries.

JazākAllāh Khayr: May God reward you the best

Khuda haafiz: May you be in God's care

Marḥūmīn: Someone who has passed away

Māshā'Allāh: As God wishes

Masjid: Mosque

Mubārak: Blessed

Musaharati: A person who beats a drum in some cultures to wake Muslims up for Suḥur

Nani: An Urdu term of Maternal Grandmother

Night of Qadr: Also known as the Night of Power is the night where the entire Qur'ān was revealed to the Prophet Muḥammad (ṣ)

Qur'ān: The holy book of Muslims

Ramaḍān: The ninth holy lunar month in the Islamic calendar, in which the Qur'ān was revealed. Muslims all around the world fast in the month of Ramaḍān

Salāmun 'alaykum: Peace be upon you

Samosa: A fried triangle-shaped pastry with a savoury filling, such as spiced potatoes, onions, peas, lentils or minced meat.

Shahr: The Arabic word for month

Suḥur: A pre-dawn meal eaten by Muslims before beginning their fast

Sūrah: A chapter of the Qur 'ān

Tawfīq: Divine blessings from God that give one the opportunity and ability to thrive toward success

Wa 'alaykum salām: And peace be upon you too

'Ulamā': Scholars

The Great Prophets Series

The Great Prophets bundle includes 5 board books, each featuring a heartwarming story about each of the `Ulul`Azm Prophets. Your toddlers will love gazing at the vibrant illustrations as they are introduced to the best of creations. These board books are perfect for little ones to hold as stories are read to them!

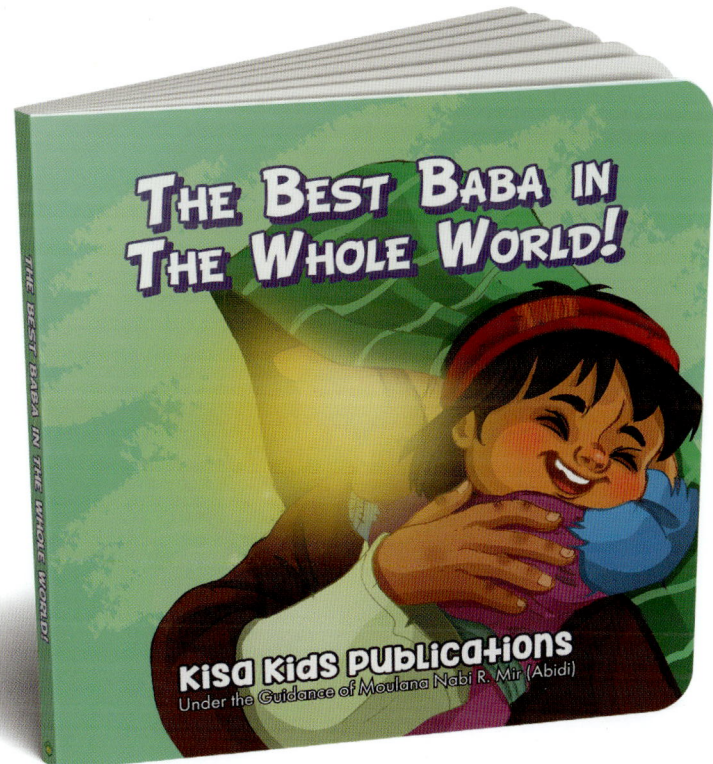 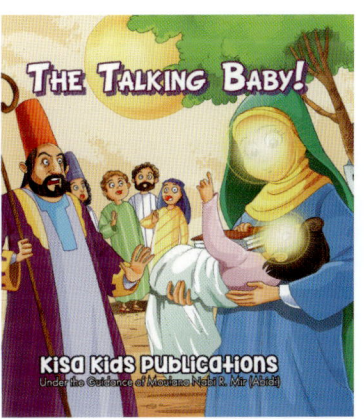 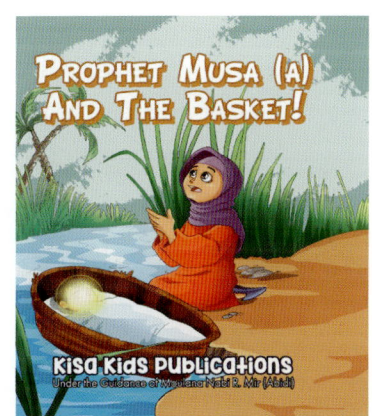 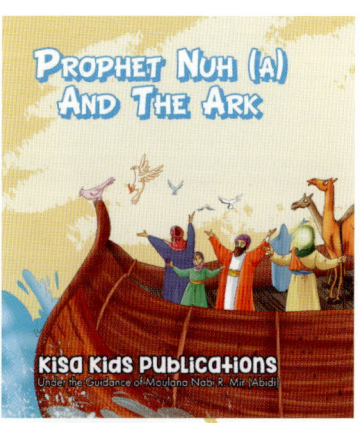 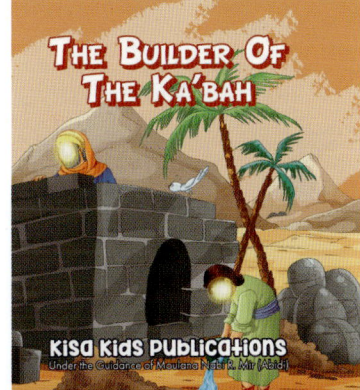 

Visit KisaKids.org to see all our products!

Rahmah The Raindrop

This is a story about Rahmah the raindrop who is swept away by the wind as she is falling into the ocean. Now, Rahmah needs to find her way back to the ocean! Along the way, she meets a little seed, a rose bush, and a bird. They all need Rahmah's help! Will Rahmah be able to help them and find her way to the ocean?

More from Kisa Kids Publications:

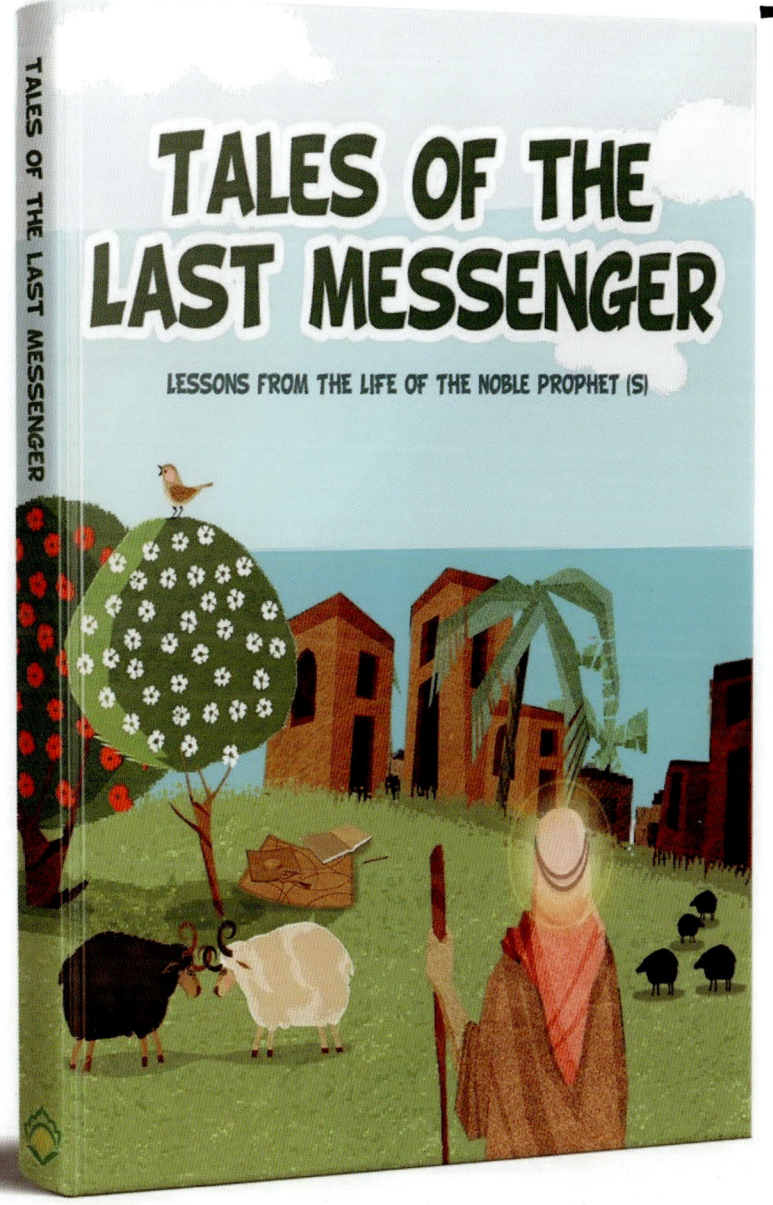

Tales of the Last Messenger

This best-seller is a collection of over 65 short stories from the life of Muḥammad, the final Prophet of Islam. Each story contains discussion points with an important takeaway message regarding ethical behavior. The goal of this book is for children to learn about the importance and methods of developing and displaying good character after reading about the personality of the Prophet Muḥammad.

My Family

Alhamdulillah

Allahu Akbar

Best time for making Dua!
when it's raining
Friday near Maghrib
Whilst fasting